D0422025

ADDITIONAL ADVANCE PRAISE FOR
HABIT CHANGERS

"M. J. shares with the world the wisdom she's gifted me over the past fifteen years. She elegantly translates her deep knowledge and experience into simple strategies that changed my work and my life."

—Patrick Burke, vice president of
Aon Health Exchanges

"M. J. Ryan taught me that my role is not that of some hyperactive musical genius, trying to play each instrument better than everyone else in the orchestra, but as the conductor, coaxing the best talents into delivering outstanding performances. This book is her distilled wisdom."

—Patrick Allman-Ward, CEO of Dana Gas

"M. J. Ryan distills complicated scientific research into actionable strategies that can be put to immediate use by anyone. M. J. demystifies the neuroscience of how we form habits and, importantly, how we each have the power to choose our own preferred behaviors—and how to elicit them in others. She's had a transformative impact on my life, and in *Habit Changers* she'll do the same for you."

—Amy Webb, founder and CEO of
Future Today Institute

HABIT CHANGERS

ALSO BY M. J. RYAN

HABIT CHANGERS

81 GAME-CHANGING MANTRAS TO MINDFULLY REALIZE YOUR GOALS

M. J. RYAN

CROWN
BUSINESS
NEW YORK

Crown Business books are available at special discounts for
bulk purchases for sales promotions or corporate use.
Special editions, including personalized covers, excerpts of
existing books, or books with corporate logos, can be created
in large quantities for special needs. For more information,
contact Premium Sales at (212) 572-2232 or e-mail
specialmarkets@penguinrandomhouse.com.

Library of Congress Cataloging-in-Publication Data
Names: Ryan, M. J. (Mary Jane), 1952– author.
Title: Habit changers : 81 game-changing mantras to mindfully
    realize your goals / M.J. Ryan.
Description: New York : Crown Business, 2016.
Identifiers: LCCN 2016005743 (print) | LCCN 2016023627 (ebook) |
    ISBN 9780451495402 (hardback) | ISBN 9780451495419 (ebook)
Subjects: LCSH: Self-actualization (Psychology) | Mindfulness
    (Psychology) | Life skills. | BISAC: BUSINESS & ECONOMICS /
    Motivational. | SELF-HELP / Personal Growth / Success.
Classification: LCC BF637.S4 .R92 2016 (print) |
    LCCN BF637.S4 (ebook) | DDC 158.1—dc23
LC record available at https://lccn.loc.gov/2016005743

ISBN 978-0-451-49540-2
eBook ISBN 978-0-451-49541-9

Printed in the United States of America

Book design by Andrea Lau
Jacket design by Kalena Schoen

10 9 8 7 6 5 4 3 2 1

First Edition

To all those seeking an easier way
to make positive changes in their lives

CONTENTS

INTRODUCTION TO
HABIT CHANGERS

What would *you* like to change in your life? Would you like to be more focused at work? Communicate more effectively? Have the time to strategize for the long term rather than simply putting out fires every day? Have greater work-life balance? Be more faithful to your health and fitness goals? Be more patient with your team or family? Have greater self-confidence? Less stress? Just . . . be *happier*? What if you could take control of your destiny and change your behavior, permanently, in ways that would help you become both happier *and* more successful?

The good news is you *can* change to have more of what you want. I know because I help people change every day. Nothing is more satisfying to me than to see someone articulate a goal and achieve it. I've been obsessed my whole life with the human potential to transform, to become happier and more successful in the ways we want to be. That's why, for the past fourteen years, I've worked with executive clients at some of the biggest companies in the world, as well as entrepreneurs and individuals from sixteen to seventy-five. I've written many books on growing positive qualities. And I give speeches and workshops on these topics around the world.

Through this work I've been privileged to watch people learn to deal better with their anger; stop worrying; become more emotionally intelligent; be more caring, confident, and powerful leaders; delegate and influence more successfully ... achieve whatever it is that they want to develop in themselves.

One thing I've learned from all my work with clients is that behavioral change is hard, regardless of how accomplished or smart or disciplined you are. You probably know that as well. You vow to change, but your best intentions end up in the rubble of your deeply ingrained habits over and over again. So you vow again—"for real this time"—but find yourself a week or a month or a year later in exactly the same spot—only more discouraged than ever.

I get it. I used to be the same way. Then I had a wake-up call. I'd been reading about a Tibetan Buddhist mind training called Lojong, or slogan practice, a set of fifty-nine one-line aphorisms you recite as antidotes to undesired mental habits. You start with the first, recite it until it becomes so ingrained that you no longer need it, then go to the second. *Hmm*, I thought, *I wonder if this kind of practice could be useful for my clients*. But I found the slogans so obscure that I didn't think they could be useful unless you're really steeped in Buddhist philosophy, so I abandoned the idea.

Or I thought I did. Apparently the concept was still rolling around in my head when one day I was working with a busy executive who was trying to learn how to get great performance from his employees without micromanaging. I was yammering on and he looked at me and said, "I'm busy. I need it boiled down to something simple so I can remember."

Without thinking, I replied, "I am going to give you a slogan. Every time you talk to an employee, say to yourself: *Give what and why, not how*." And so he did.

His transformation was instantaneous and astonishing. Because the slogan was so simple, he could actually easily remember to repeat it—over and over again. And each time he did, he was able to instruct his employees in a constructive way rather than micromanaging. His boss and employees all noticed the change, and within three months he received the promotion to director that had eluded him for years. As we finished our work together, he thanked me for what he described as a powerful course correction that he had not been able to pinpoint before.

It was then that I realized I could use the principle of slogan practice to help *all* of my clients, and many others too, by creating memorable one-line phrases that would serve as the *habit changers* they needed. I started coming up with phrases for the things they wanted to remember to do or be, and it turned out the simple act of repeating these over and over worked for them as well. Without exception, people found it easier to enact the change they wanted.

WHY HABIT CHANGERS WORK

How can it be, you might ask, that the simple act of repeating a one-line slogan can actually produce real, meaningful, and lasting behavioral change? Recent findings in neuroscience explain why these little reminders are so effective. To conserve energy, the brain creates habits of thinking and acting that become automatic. Such habits operate from the basal ganglia, the unconscious part of your mind, which means they are mostly invisible to you. This thinking is automatic, even as it dictates most of what we do all day. This is great when you're brushing your teeth or driving your car. Who would want to have to figure that out every day?

But when it comes to something habitual that you want to change, your unconsciousness is precisely the problem. Without consciousness, you can't choose differently. That's why you find yourself thinking after the fact, *I wasn't going to eat a cupcake in the afternoon!* Or *I was going to stand up for myself in that meeting.* Or *I wasn't going to yell at her. It just happened!* You end up doing the same old thing, not because you're weak but because you're on automatic pilot. The one-liners in this book work because they override that automatic system, help you become *consciously* aware of what you're doing—and serve as a reminder of what it is that you want to do. From a brain perspective, they are helping you transfer control of your behavior from the basal ganglia to the prefrontal cortex, your brain's executive center. Here you have awareness and therefore choice, and from here you can act differently. You can notice what you are about to do and recall what you *want* to do—instead of just launching unthinkingly into your old habit.

Awareness is crucial to change, because initially, learning is all about awareness. "In the 1960s, psychologists identified three stages that we pass through in the acquisition of new skills," states science writer Joshua Foer in *Maximize Your Potential*. "We start in the 'cognitive phase,' during which we're intellectualizing the task, discovering new strategies to perform better, and making lots of mistakes. We're consciously focusing on what we're doing. Then we enter the 'associative stage,' when we're making fewer errors, and gradually getting better. Finally, we arrive at the 'autonomous stage,' when we turn on autopilot and move the skill to the back of our proverbial mental filing cabinet and stop paying it conscious attention." Repeating these habit changers helps you practice enough in the conscious and the associative stages that new behavior eventually gets programmed into the autonomous stage.

The Asaro tribe of Indonesia and Papua New Guinea have a beautiful saying that describes what we need to do when learning something new: "Knowledge is only a rumor until it lives in the muscle." We have to go beyond good intentions and do the new behavior over and over till we build the muscle of the habit. The habit changer you choose will help you do that.

That's not to say that intention is not powerful. According to Rick Hanson and Richard Mendius in their book *Buddha's Brain*, our "brains evolved from the bottom up and the inside out, along what is called the *neuroaxis*." When we create positive intentions, "they ripple up and down the neuroaxis" throughout all parts of our brain to fulfill those intentions. What this means is that when we decide to use a habit changer, we set off powerful mechanisms in our brain to create and support the change we desire. And if we stick to it long enough, we can permanently change our brain for the better.

How long is long enough? Till you are in the autonomous stage—when you no longer have to think about it; you just do it. And despite those optimistic books that promise "seven days to change a habit," it takes a lot of practice. It varies from person to person, but six to nine months seems to be the average time it takes to build a new pathway. The old habit is still there too, which is why under stress we can find ourselves going back to our prior behavior. But when stress kicks in is when habit changers are the most powerful—they can help you avoid that trap and quickly steer you back to your new behavior.

Some people have asked me if these phrases are

affirmations. Absolutely not. Affirmations proclaim that you already possess a quality you are trying to achieve: "I am calm," "I am confident," etc. I personally think such statements are worthless because somewhere inside you know they're a lie—you're not calm and confident, and by lying to yourself, you're only creating a greater awareness of your lack, making change feel more unattainable.

Rather, I call these phrases habit changers and define them as "a newly introduced element or factor that changes an existing situation or activity in a significant way." Because unlike affirmations, these one-liners are more than reminders—they are actually the *instructions* for change. More than a prompt to take your medicine, they are the medicine itself. By thinking or saying them, you're actually training your mind to enact your intention. Many of my clients call them mantras. They are like the Hindu definition of a mantra, which is a sacred verbal formula, because they are short phrases you repeat over and over. But unlike a true mantra, which is said to cause spiritual transformation in and of itself, these phrases work on a neural level, reminding you how you want to behave and so making it easier to live into the change.

HOW TO USE HABIT CHANGERS

This book can do for you what it has done for my clients: allow you to successfully implement the changes you want in your life simply by repeating these short, memorable phrases. If it sounds astonishingly simple, that's because it is—and it's also astonishingly effective. In this book you'll find the eighty-one phrases that my clients have found most useful, grouped in the table of contents by the issue they address. To begin, scan the table of contents for what you want to focus on. Pick one topic, not ten—or even two. It's the single-pointed focus that makes this work. Once you've created and sustained the first new habit you desire, you can work with another phrase.

For whichever change you've chosen, you'll see the habit changers and explanatory text. Choose the phrase that resonates the most with you and feel free to adapt it so it feels just right for you and your situation. I've noticed that some people refer to themselves as "me" and others "you." As in: "Now come back to me" versus "Now come back to you." Make it work for you. Turn it into a question if that feels better—some clients tell me that as statements they find the habit changers lifeless, but as questions they are intriguing. It is a matter of how your mind processes information, so do what feels right to you. There's no way to be wrong with this.

Once you get accustomed to the practice, feel free to make up your own habit changer or use a saying from somewhere else that resonates for you. My sister told me a wonderful story recently of how she uses "little by little," a phrase said to her by her Cuban mother-in-law, to remind herself not to get overwhelmed by the big picture and to just take things slow and steady. "I can still hear her whispering it to me in her Spanish accent when I start to freeze at the enormity of a task," she told me.

Copy the phrase out and put it where you can see it night and day—more than one place if needed—on your mirror, in the car, on your iPhone. In the beginning, external reminders help us activate our intention and practice enough to build the habit.

To give your phrase even more power, add in a visual image and a gesture. For "This person is my teacher," for instance, perhaps bring to mind an image of a teacher you've had whom you really appreciated, and turn your hands slightly outward to receive the learning. For "Anger is fear on the boil," maybe bring to mind a teakettle and use your hand to turn down the flame. These are just suggestions—you need to use whatever image and gesture come to your mind. When you add an image and a gesture, you enhance your learning because you are activating all three of your perceptual channels—auditory (the phrase), visual (the image), and kinesthetic (the gesture). Many of us refer to ourselves as "auditory" or "visual" or "kinesthetic" learners, but we actually need all three inputs to learn most effectively.

Recent research into gestures shows how powerful they can be in affecting our mood and behavior. Two minutes in the Wonder Woman pose—hands on hips, feet spread apart, slight smile—can raise your testosterone levels up to 20 percent and reduce cortisol, one of the stress hormones, by 20 percent, leaving you feeling more assertive and calm all day long. And you don't need to spend two minutes. According to a 2012 study by scientists Pablo Briñol, Richard Petty, and Benjamin Wagner, simply standing straight, with shoulders back and spine erect (what they call a "confident posture"), led people to rate themselves more confidently than people in a "doubtful posture," slumped and self-contained. And self-compassion research by Kristin Neff, associate professor of human development and culture at the University of Texas at Austin, shows that when we put a hand (or both) on the center of our chest, we feel soothed and comforted, as if we've been hugged by someone who cares about us. Our brains release oxytocin, a hormone that reduces anxiety and creates feelings of contentment, calmness, and security.

You can take advantage of these learnings to make your phrases more powerful: Add a power pose to the habit changers on risk taking, self-confidence, boundaries, and resilience—anytime you need a bit more oomph. Put your hand on your chest for the ones on fear, worry, stress, acceptance—anytime you need a bit of soothing.

As you begin to use your habit changer, don't expect to do it perfectly. Be kind to yourself when you forget your phrase or when you say it but can't enact it. Harsh judgment doesn't create positive change. However, being gentle with ourselves when we blow it isn't always easy to do. As Neff's self-compassion research explains it, the amygdala, a part of our brain that we share with all animals from reptiles upward, exists to turn on the fight-or-flight response when it perceives a threat. When we decide to change something in ourselves and fail to do it perfectly, the amygdala perceives that as a threat and beats us up in order to "help" us fight the threat. That's why we think being hard on ourselves is useful. Neff has shown, however, that such an instinctive response works against us. Rather, to produce the change we want to see, it's much better to engage another part of our brain—the attach system. This is our tendency to soothe and be compassionate. When we treat ourselves with self-compassion and get that hit of oxytocin, Neff has discovered, we're more able to recover from our "failure" and sustain the change we want.

You *will* blow it. I have too. Here's just one example: I'd been using the phrase "My response is my responsibility" to remind myself that I am account-able for my response rather than blame whatever or whoever has triggered it. As a result, I'd been calmer in traffic and nicer to my husband. We enjoyed a bliss-ful tiff-free stretch of three months. Then one day he said something and I totally lost it. I forgot that I was going to focus on *my* response and just let him have it in great self-righteous indignation that lasted a full twelve hours. After I cleaned up the emotional mess and apologized to him, I had to forgive myself for for-getting my habit changer and get right back at it.

Like me, you'll mess up every now and again. But as long as you treat yourself as you would a young child learning to walk—encouragingly—and keep on trying, the new behavior will get easier. It doesn't matter how many times you blow it. The more you use your phrase, the more ingrained it will become in your brain and the easier it will become to live it.

Our capacity to consciously change is our greatest gift as human beings. I truly hope that, whatever it is you desire to grow in yourself, these habit changers will help—that they will help transform you, as they have my clients, into the happy, powerful, caring, and successful leader and person you desire to be. I know you can do it! So let's get started.

Acceptance

People
do what
people
always do

Do you find yourself surprised, frustrated, or angry when the people close to you behave in the same dysfunctional way over and over? I often work with people on leadership teams who are frustrated by one another and shocked when their leader or colleagues act the same way over and over. Each time is a fresh new affront. As you know, at least in theory, trying to change another person can be exhausting—and impossible! So why make yourself crazy trying? I coined this phrase decades ago for a friend who was all worked up about how someone else kept behaving. But why, I asked, did she expect anything else? People do what people always do. Yes, your mother will criticize everything you do, yes, your coworker will be crabby in the morning, and yes, your child will leave trash in your car. People don't generally change very much, despite our desire for them to do so. And when they do, it generally comes from a deep-seated inner longing, certainly not because you want them to. If they do change for us, it tends to be a pasted-on, short-lived endeavor. There is simply no point in trying to change others. Instead, when we surrender to the truth that they will do what they always do, we don't have to be so disappointed, frustrated, angry, or annoyed when they continue to be exactly who they are. It creates not only acceptance but also greater peace of mind.

This person is my teacher

This is a practice that comes from Buddhism. It's about seeing everyone who annoys, frustrates, angers, or otherwise bothers you as someone who is providing you the opportunity to grow some positive quality in yourself—your equanimity, your kindness, your patience, your boundaries, your tolerance.... It's up to you to figure out what you're supposed to be learning. It's a way to stop focusing on what the other person is doing that bothers you and instead concentrate on what your reaction to that person is trying to teach you about yourself. A brave young leader I was working with used it with a direct report of his who was driving him crazy. His first impulse was to complain about this person at every coaching session. But when I suggested that he see this problematic person as his teacher, he took the idea on wholeheartedly and said, "Well, I guess he's here to teach me to be more patient and precise in my managing, because he is always asking me to clarify what I mean when I think I've already made myself clear." That perspective enabled him to give his employee more of what he needed, and their working relationship got better as a result. The leader found this habit changer so helpful that he used it with every problematic person he came across—and grew exponentially as a result.

You're
where
you're
supposed
to be

Roberto was in a jam. In the process of moving his family from one town to another, he'd lost his job. To afford the mortgage, he needed a job pronto. He started applying to all sorts of places, including "ones I would never have even considered before," as he told me later. He ended up getting hired by a company he didn't think highly of at the time. "But it turned out to be the best move I could have made. It provided me with both stability—I've been there ten years—and flexibility—the chance to work at home to be available for my kids while they were growing up. I learned that I was where I was supposed to be, and I've used that saying to help me accept other situations gracefully. When I had to do the evening routine with my two kids (including the cooking) every weekday for years because my wife was working nights, for instance, or having to drive half an hour round-trip to help my ninety-year-old mother-in-law work her remote—again!—it's helped me keep my cool over and over. What's interesting is that now that my kids are grown and the situation at work has changed, it's no longer where I am supposed to be—and so I am looking for a new job."

Anger

Anger is
fear on
the boil

L ike a lot of my high-powered clients, anger was an issue for me when I was younger. I never got mad at work, only at home. I'd try extremely hard to be perfect and bite my tongue, and then something would set me off and—kaboom!—I'd explode at my significant other. One day early on in my relationship with my now husband, I lost my temper. Instead of getting angry back or walking out, he asked me, "What are you afraid of?" That was the moment I understood that under anger there is always fear. Fear of not getting our needs met, fear of failure, fear of . . . fill in the blank. That's why I resonated so strongly when I read a version of this phrase in Caitlin Moran's novel *How to Build a Girl*. Since then, clients have used this habit changer when they're mad to remind themselves that underneath their fire is some kind of fear. Understanding that—and perhaps even expressing the fear instead of the anger—can change the situation for the better. At least you'll know what the need is that you're trying to satisfy! A senior executive used it to help her recognize what was going on for her when she got mad in meetings, so she could tell her colleagues that she was afraid of failing if they didn't pull together as a leadership team. They appreciated her vulnerability much more than the hostility they had been getting previously. The team dynamics improved as a result.

Stop, breathe, rewind

Jessica was one of my clients who had anger issues. Her blowups were so frequent that they were threatening to derail her career. I taught her that anger is the fight response of the fight-or-flight mechanism. It occurs when the amygdala, the center of the "threat" system of the brain, perceives a possible danger and hijacks the prefrontal cortex, the more rational part of our brain. The trick to anger management is to recognize when you've been hijacked and not act from that place. It's easier said than done because your amygdala is screaming for you to fight. I taught Jessica to recognize the signs when she was hijacked, which for her came in the form of starting to feel hot and tight in her body. I suggested that as soon as she felt that way, she should imagine a bright red stop sign in front of her and think, *Stop. Breathe. Rewind*, while taking slow, deep breaths through her nose and relaxing her body as much as possible. Stopping and breathing fools the amygdala into relaxing a bit, reducing the sense of threat and bringing the prefrontal cortex back online. The rewind is to get you back to what was happening before you started to feel threatened, so you have a chance to react more logically. It worked for Jessica—and I've been using it with clients ever since.

This anger
is false
advertising

To my mind, anger comes in two forms. One is righteous anger—there is an issue that is unjust—and you feel your passion rise to do something about it. That's healthy anger. The other is fear, that sense of threat that comes from the amygdala, which was originally designed to alert you to a present *physical* danger. If the danger is real—you are about to be attacked on the street—that's also healthy anger. But because the threat mechanism comes from that ancient part of our brain, the part that, as I once read, is fully developed in humans by the age of two, it's not very sophisticated. It often senses threats and cuts off access to our higher thinking even when there is no true physical danger but rather "threats" from other people that it determined to be bad when we were very young. Thus it works against us a lot of the time, because when we're dealing with interpersonal problems, we don't want to be reacting from our toddler amygdala. This habit changer can help you recognize that most likely what you're getting angry about is a false threat. In other words, you're not in any immediate physical danger. It's your amygdala's false advertising, as I like to call it. This doesn't mean what is threatening you isn't an issue to deal with, just that once you recognize it's not a matter of life or death by repeating the phrase "This anger is false advertising," you can calm down and respond from your most mature thinking. It's saved a lot of clients from childish outbursts and can do the same for you, as well.

Authenticity

You are as
you are
evidenced

I once worked with Alice, a woman who needed to grow her authenticity as a leader. She was coming across as phony in her interactions, and as a result, her colleagues didn't trust her. Several referred to her as the "Stepford employee," after the movie *The Stepford Wives*, in which women are replaced by robots. It was a big wake-up call to get this feedback from her colleagues. She had no idea they were seeing her in this way. She had been trying so hard to do her job perfectly that it was coming across as very formulaic. At first she wanted to blame the people giving the feedback, but because it was something many folks felt, she bravely accepted that this was how she was perceived. In helping her to figure out how to come across more true to who she was inside, I recalled something a friend of mine, sales strategist Beatrice Stonebanks, once said: "You are as you are evidenced." I suggested Alice repeat it before she met with anyone, to remind her of how she wanted to come across. She found it a very helpful reminder that showing up as you intend means others will see you as intended. That, along with getting more comfortable revealing her true feelings—including being honest about what she didn't know—enabled her to come across as her true self, which had a positive effect on her relationship with her colleagues. Use this habit changer to make sure you are projecting the you that you want others to see. Because ultimately that is the you that you are.

Walk your
own path

ophia was in a bind. She had a wonderful idea for a business that she was genuinely passionate about. She had the freedom in her life to pursue it and, because of an unexpected inheritance, the capital to start. So what was the problem? She was afraid of what "they" would say if her idea didn't pan out. Have you ever been in a similar situation? So concerned about what other people might think or say that you were paralyzed? And who are these mysterious "they" who have such a hold over our lives, anyway? Whenever I work with folks in situations like Sophia's, that's the first question I ask. Sometimes people can pinpoint a person or group they are concerned with impressing, but most often the fear stems from an amorphous sense of others watching and passing judgment on our actions. My hunch is that our concern about this comes from our amygdala, that toddler part of our brain that in this case is trying to keep us safe by not standing out from the crowd. Unfortunately that instinct works against our taking the kinds of risks that might bring us the greatest satisfaction and sense of fulfillment. When I explained this to Sophia, she agreed and then said, "I need to walk my own path." We agreed that she'd use that phrase to encourage herself when she got too caught up in what "they" might think. And she walked her own path to a thriving business with ten employees.

Blame

First correct, then prevent

Lucy, a manager of a team that was working on creating a very complex product on a very tight deadline, was typical of many clients I've worked with. When a problem arose, she'd bring her team together, ostensibly to fix the situation. However, she'd quickly go into blame mode, trying to figure out whose fault it was. Her team would get defensive in response, throwing one another or people in other parts of the organization under the bus to deflect her wrath. A tremendous amount of time was lost. What she needed to do instead was to solve the immediate burning problem, then go back later and figure out how to prevent such issues from reoccurring. This was a lesson I learned early on in my previous career as a book publisher. When a crisis hits, fix it. Don't waste time analyzing why or who. Then afterward solve for the pattern, so it doesn't happen again. If you try to do both at the same time, you do neither well. Another client of mine put it this way: "First correct, then prevent." *Bingo!* I thought. *That's it!* I gave this habit changer to Lucy, who has used it ever since when things go awry, which, given the nature of what she does, is often. As a result, her group has gotten faster at solving the immediate burning platform—and preventing future fires.

A pointed
finger is
a victim's
logo

I love this saying by Joseph Brodsky. And it once provided a big wake-up call for a client of mine. Jeff was someone who, in his own mind, could do no wrong. No matter what happened, he wasn't to blame. That meant, of course, that he was an expert at deflecting responsibility onto others whenever a problem arose: "It wasn't me because I'm not in charge of that" was his standard response. His behavior was a problem because he worked in a large, matrixed organization where people needed to share accountability. At first he didn't recognize that he was the problem. In fact, in each of these situations he saw himself as victorious and the others as the victims of his superior maneuvering. One day I asked him if he'd ever heard the Brodsky quote. He said he hated anyone who acted like a victim and it was the last thing he ever wanted to be. I challenged him to see that that was how he was coming across, and he decided to use this habit changer in the hope it could transform his habit. And it has—to a great degree. Sometimes he still blames others and shirks accountability, but he's gotten better at recognizing what he's done, apologizing, and making sure the lines of responsibility are clarified going forward.

My response
is my
responsibility

This one's for you if, like me, you think it's the other person's fault when you get angry, annoyed, or frustrated—if you think: *You made me mad*, *It's your fault I'm so upset*, or *If you hadn't ___ then I wouldn't have ___*. Despite years of therapy and communication training, it's taken me many decades to really get that my response is my responsibility. That doesn't mean that the other person didn't do whatever is it I'm worked up about but rather that I alone am responsible for my reaction. Which means that if I get worked up, I need to deal with my reaction within myself until I've cooled down enough to decide whether this is an issue that needs to be addressed with the other person. Because it is only when I am calm that I can talk about it in a way that does no damage to me, the other person, or our relationship. Otherwise I'm likely to say or do things that are mean or destructive because the "fight" of the fight-or-flight response has taken control of my brain. This is the habit changer that truly changed my life. Since I started using it, I've become much less volatile and blaming, which has done wonders for my twenty-three-year marriage— and the likelihood of its lasting at least twenty-three years more! Give it a try if you find yourself playing the blame game at work or at home. You are responsible for your response, and it's up to you to be as skillful in responding as possible.

Boundaries

B

Whose business is this?

Do you often find yourself feeling responsible for other people's behavior? Do you try to control other people's reactions at work or at home? Have you found yourself rescuing others by doing their work for them? Making others look more responsible? seem more approachable? sound more reasonable? Some of my clients take on the shortcomings of their prickly or less productive colleagues, clients, or family members and try to cover, prevent, or solve other people's problems for them. Although this is more common among my female clients, men can do it too. If this behavior sounds familiar, you may have trouble with boundaries. In these circumstances I prescribe this question from spiritual teacher Byron Katie. She says there are three types of "business" in the world: God's (floods, earthquakes, and other random acts of nature), yours (you and your response to what life presents to you), and theirs (what is the other person's to handle and respond to). I used this habit changer when my daughter became a teenager and was in pain over finding her place in the world. It helped remind me that I can support her, I can care deeply, but her business is hers to sort out. Clients have used the same habit changer with peers, bosses, spouses, siblings.... It's useful in *any* relationship where you are overinvolved.

Now come
back to me

I'm currently working with three women on a leadership team who are highly empathetic and get easily caught up in other people's feelings. It's a small management team, and they are close, but this intimacy sometimes works against them when they lose portions of their workday over something that's happened in the life of one member of the trio. One gets upset, and the other two swoop in to tend and befriend and soon find themselves upset over the first person's upset. If this has ever happened to you with a colleague, friend, child, or other person, you know what it feels like. Suddenly you are swamped by someone else's feelings and concerns, and you lose not only perspective on the situation but also any sense of what *you* want or feel. Your life becomes not truly your own because you are living other people's feelings instead of your own. This is caused, according to Richard Davidson, professor of psychology at the University of Wisconsin at Madison, by overactive social intuition combined with slow-to-recover resilience. This habit changer will help you modulate that. It will allow you to go over and care for the person and then remember to come back to yourself so that you are inside of you and experiencing your own life. Try putting your hand on your heart as you repeat the phrase, which will further help you come back to yourself.

You can't
say yes if
you can't
say no

I was once working with an executive director of a nonprofit. Part of the coaching process entails going out after the session and trying the new behavior we've discussed, but after a few sessions I noticed she was skipping that part. Every time we met, she'd agree to do it, but when we met next time, she hadn't done it. I realized I needed to gently point that out to her. When I did, she had an epiphany: "That's why people are so upset with me as a leader! I do that with everyone—I say yes to whatever they ask because I want to please them, and then I don't follow through because I've got too much to do!" Sound familiar? Are you someone who can't say no? It stems from a desire to make others happy and avoid conflict, but it ends up creating more conflict and disappointment than if you had said no in the first place. Here's the reality: You can't really say yes if you can't say no. That's because when you say yes to something you can't follow through on, you're not actually being helpful—you're just appeasing those around you and ultimately causing bad feeling. This habit changer can really turn that around, as this client of mine can attest. She used it to remember that "yes" and "no" are two options that you have choice about. She discovered that the more she could say no when she felt it, the more her "yes" was wholehearted. Her follow-through improved dramatically, and so did her team's respect for her word.

Change

C

Build a
bridge to
the future
on the
pillars of
the past

A lot of people come to me when they are at a crossroads in their career. They've gotten into a rut and want support in breaking out of it. I take them through a process that my friend Dawna Markova, PhD, outlines in her book *I Will Not Die an Unlived Life*. It's an examination of your strengths, passions, and values, as well as the environments that bring out your best. Once they do that process, typically they experience greater clarity about what they want to do. The problem is that getting from here to there can feel like standing on one side of the Grand Canyon and trying to figure out how to get to the other side. It's easy to feel overwhelmed and stuck. That's when I give folks this habit changer. It's about remembering to leverage what you've already done to create the new. I used it to start the work I'm doing now. I leveraged my business experience as a book publisher to brand myself as an executive coach. And who were my first clients? Publishers and writers whom I knew previously. Similarly, a client of mine used this habit changer to go from being a contractor to networking computers, offering the unique service of installing the cable as well as doing the software. The point is, nothing you've done in the past is a waste. It's all grist for your future. Reminding yourself of this will help you figure out how to get from here to there.

Stop
the war
against
the way
things are

This is a phrase that comes from Thai Buddhist teacher Ajahn Chah to help us accept when change is happening rather than fight against it. It takes a lot of energy to resist reality—to complain, deny, bemoan, try to escape. It costs us time as well. Busy executives and entrepreneurs can't afford the cost of these types of behaviors. Organizational theorists claim that today, in large part because of globalization, we are living in a VUCA world—volatile, uncertain, chaotic, and ambiguous. To succeed in such a world, they maintain, the key ability we each need to cultivate is "change agility," the ability to quickly adapt when change happens. Those who can adapt swiftly, they say, will have an advantage over those stuck bemoaning the loss of the past. This habit changer can help. A CEO client of mine used it to deal with a shock that came out of the blue: He heard a rumor that the board wanted him to step down. In the past he would have spent a lot of time and energy in self-recrimination, blame, and power politics. Instead, within twenty-four hours he'd regrouped—using this slogan—and presented a plan to the board for an orderly exit that gave him a decent runway and the organization a peaceful and well-thought-out transition. As this leader demonstrated, stopping the war against the way things are frees us up to deal most effectively with the way things are!

Collaboration

C

Bake a
bigger pie

This is a concept that comes from business guru Guy Kawasaki. It's a great metaphor for the art of collaboration. Many people think that collaborating simply means agreeing with others, but in reality it's the process of jointly coming up with previously un-thought-of solutions that expand the pie to satisfy everyone. It requires open and honest communication and a focus on creative and novel solutions. People who are strong at collaborating are generally good at asking questions, listening to other points of view, and incorporating those viewpoints into expanded options. None of these behaviors described Tom. In any situation he was sure he was right and asserted this so strongly. When he felt he couldn't win, he'd fall back to a "let's split the difference" compromise position. His new role, however, required him to truly collaborate with others on innovative products, or the company would fail. Splitting the difference had resulted in products with unacceptable trade-offs of quality for speed. He agreed to use "Build a bigger pie" to help him stay focused on the goal—to come up not with merely acceptable ideas that could be executed quickly but with truly great ones that made everyone excited *and* could meet the time line. Every time his team got stuck, he'd ask, "How can we build a bigger pie?" This ultimately resulted in the creation of a whole new category-killing product that blew away the competition. What might it do for you?

Don't be "Fred"

My client was not happy. She was complaining about "Fred," a colleague who, due to a new initiative, she was going to have to work with for at least the coming year: "He never listens; he's convinced he's always right; he just pushes his solution without ever considering that ours might be better." *Hmm*, I thought. These were the very issues that had brought my client to coaching, ones that she and I had been working on for a couple of months with no great results. She understood theoretically the negative effects of her behavior but didn't feel a great motivation to change. "So you don't like what Fred's doing?" I asked. "Absolutely not," she replied. Then the penny dropped: "Oh, he's acting in exactly the way I do sometimes. Now I get what people have been complaining about. It's really obnoxious." Once she understood that Fred was a mirror to her, I suggested that she use "Don't be Fred" to remind herself of how she didn't want to behave. It worked like a charm. I invite you to use it when you find yourself in situations that call on you to be as effective as possible, substituting, of course, the name of someone who deeply annoys you. Even if you don't believe you're anything like that person, using him or her as a negative example can spur you to be at your best.

Be a
yea-sayer

ulia was a brilliant thinker who came to me because, she said, no one wanted to work with her. When I probed more deeply, I understood what seemed to be the problem. She had an incredible talent for seeing the potential flaws in any proposed plan or idea. "That won't work because . . ." was her favorite phrase. In describing her response to an initiative a colleague had suggested, she told me she had said, "Can't anyone else smell what stinks in here?" I helped her see that her talent could be very useful—if she learned to refine her presentation. Her objections were true and important, but people just saw her as a naysayer, which made her a person to avoid and ignore. She quickly understood that this was a problem but was having trouble figuring out what to say instead. "You've got to first be a yea-sayer," I suggested. "Think about what you can appreciate or agree with in what they are saying. Then ask if they would like your help in analyzing the idea to make it more effective." Pointing out only what was wrong was a deeply grooved habit for her, but the more she told herself to "be a yea-sayer, be a yea-sayer" in meetings, the more she found ways to build on and strengthen other people's ideas rather than just try to kill them. Pretty soon her team went from ignoring her to asking her to point out the flaws in their ideas and suggest how to overcome them. She learned to properly balance yea- and naysaying—and that made all the difference in her ability to collaborate.

Accept the offer and move it forward

This is a concept that comes from improvisational theater. When doing improv, your job is to respond to whatever comes at you and not just roll with it but take it somewhere new before tossing it to the next person, who will develop the concept further. It's great practice in cultivating your creativity, spontaneity, listening, and collaboration. In fact, many improv theaters offer corporate workshops for that very reason. I first gave this as a habit changer to my client George. He came to me because he had "trouble collaborating," according to his stakeholders. When I watched him interact, it was clear he didn't know how to build on other people's ideas. He had his own ideas, which he advocated for; if people didn't like them, he would simply withdraw. I explained that collaboration was the art of developing ideas together, not a duel with a winner and a loser. I knew he liked baseball, so I told him it was like catching the ball in the glove, moving it to the other hand, and then throwing it onward. He used that image, along with the slogan and a tiny hand gesture that represented the ball catch, to get better at acknowledging others' ideas and building on them. Use this habit changer to improve your ability to generate more creative ideas with others.

Surprise is the enemy of trust

ick needed to learn to collaborate more effectively, his manager explained to me. He wasn't communicating enough with his stakeholders, and it was hurting their ability to work well together in areas that overlapped. Rick wasn't purposely withholding information. It was just that he was a new hire in a large organization who'd come from a small company where he'd always operated autonomously, and he simply didn't see a need to explain what he was doing. But especially in large, matrixed organizations, where decisions are often made through the capacity to get buy-in for your ideas from multiple stakeholders, the Lone Ranger approach rarely works. People get suspicious that you are trying to pull something over on them or compete against them. Rick was willing to learn to share information; he just kept forgetting to communicate his thoughts to stakeholders. He would show up at a leadership team meeting with a fully baked idea, which the others proceeded to shoot down because it didn't align with what they were doing. I gave him this habit changer to help him figure out who he needed to vet the idea with before the meeting to get input and alignment. "It's amazing what letting people know in advance does," he reported later to me. "Not only are they then not surprised, but my original idea gets even better when people who've been here longer help me navigate the system." Use it when you need to remember to communicate to collaborate!

Communication

C

Talking
and
listening
should be
practiced
in equal
measure

I wouldn't call this a specialty exactly, but I often work with very articulate folks who are very good on broadcast mode but not so good at listening. They're the ones who invite someone to a meeting, talk the entire time, then leave, saying, "Good meeting," without the other person ever having opened their mouth. It's extremely frustrating for those around them, who can't get a word in edgewise. This overtalking is generally not conscious, however. In fact, they are often shocked when presented with evidence of how much they spoke in a meeting. (Yes, I've timed people to help them get the message!) Carol was such a person. Once I revealed her ratio of talking to listening, she was embarrassed and committed to change. She put a red sticky that represented this habit changer on her phone to remind her to pause and listen after every time she said something—and to talk in sentences, not paragraphs, before listening. Listening was hard, she confessed. She had to fight the urge to burst in with her response. But, using this phrase, her listening skills got noticeably better. If you suspect you might need help with this, time your ratio of talking to listening. If it's out of whack, use this habit changer to help you zip your lip. You will be amazed what you'll hear simply by listening more.

Ask,
don't
tell

Jenn was, in her own words, "very direct." Translation: She had no problem telling everyone—direct reports, peers, even those above her—what to do. Behind her back people called her the "little general"; everyone tried to escape when she came into a room. I helped her see that her command-and-control style of leadership was only one possible leadership strategy, best used sparingly and only in emergencies because it's so disempowering. "When the building is on fire, ordering people around is crucial," I explained. "But otherwise you need to learn other ways of communicating: through inspiration, vision, coaching, empathizing with people's feelings, et cetera." We began to work on those new strategies, and she did improve, but only somewhat. Her spirit was willing, but her habit of bossing people around was very strong. So one day I said, "You know the military's former 'Don't ask, don't tell' policy? Well, here's your new policy: Ask, don't tell. When you want someone to do something, ask, 'Would you be willing to spearhead this?' rather than saying, 'You must do this.'" "Okay," she said. This little adjustment has helped her a lot—in ways neither of us could have seen at the outset. Just the other day she said to me, "Whenever I open my mouth, I just say to myself, *Ask, don't tell,* and I am having so much more success, not only with my employees and coworkers but my family as well!"

Headline
first

I've gotten feedback dozens of times that I have 'communication issues' and should learn to get to the point faster," Bob said when we first started working together. "I've had all kinds of coaching but it hasn't really changed." "What if I told you that I don't think there's anything wrong with you?" I asked. That got his attention. I explained that I believed that, based on how his mind processed information, he naturally spoke in metaphors and stories, and that other people whose minds worked differently from his probably couldn't track the point of the story, which is why they got frustrated. I suggested that he think of the way he spoke like a story in the newspaper. All stories have a headline. If he said the headline first, people would then understand the point and be able to appreciate his story all the way through. I gave him "Headline first" as his habit changer. It forced him to pause before speaking to figure out the point of what he wanted to say, and saying it not only helped the listeners but also helped him to stay on track. Since then, I've used this with most of my clients, because regardless of whether you have an identified problem with communication, saying the headline first helps the listener understand where you're heading. It creates a clarity that moves conversations forward.

Moderate
to resonate

A stakeholder was expressing his concern that an executive client of mine didn't consider her audience before she spoke. As a result, she often put her foot in her mouth—alienating and insulting people without awareness or intention. "She needs to be more mindful of whom she's talking to," he said. "She needs to moderate to resonate." I gave this feedback to my client, and she used the phrase to remember to think about whom she was speaking to before she spoke, which helped her overall effectiveness as a communicator. I've also suggested it to leaders who don't understand their positional power—that because of who they are in the organization what they say and how they say it sends reverberations throughout their team or division. Often the very charisma, high energy, and forcefulness that got folks to the top can be overpowering and intimidating, resulting in people being afraid to disagree, bring bad news, or otherwise communicate honestly. Because their forcefulness and high energy are so intrinsic and have served them well in their rise to the top, these leaders can have trouble understanding that such qualities can have negative effects on others. Learning to resonate with a group or an individual is a form of emotional intelligence that turns good leaders into great ones—and this phrase can help you remember to do it!

Conflict

Don't push buttons that don't need to be

My sixteen-year-old daughter said this to me one day to remind me I didn't need to give her a lecture on doing her homework. She was absolutely right. My talking would serve only to annoy her and to reduce the likelihood of her doing what I wanted her to do. Since then I've been giving this habit changer to clients like Matt who have a tendency to give long-winded lectures that are demotivating and completely unnecessary. I have sat in meetings where Matt pontificated in generalizations about the problems with "people's" behavior for ten minutes, repeating the same points over and over. No one else dared say a word. They just sat there with their heads down, waiting for the tirade to be over. I call it the "wolf and sheep dynamic." The wolf growls and shows his teeth and the sheep freeze, hoping if they stay still they won't get eaten. It accomplishes nothing whatsoever, except to alienate people and increase team turnover. When I spoke with him about it, Matt truly believed such monologues would improve his team's performance. I helped him see that he was pushing people's buttons unnecessarily. He used this habit changer to edit his lecturing tendency and instead to think, *What do I want people to do?* then simply suggest or request that, rather than beat them over the head with it.

Presume goodwill

It's so easy to get upset or angry at someone and conclude he's a nasty person who's just out to challenge or harm you, isn't it? When someone acts in a way you don't like, it's only human to make assumptions about his intentions and motivations. We say, "It's only human," because the human brain is structured to take in information, draw conclusions from that information based on our previous history, and then act on the basis of those assumptions, a process that is largely unconscious. Experts describe it this way: We push the present through a filter based on the past in order to predict the future. Unfortunately, these conclusions get in the way of creating and maintaining healthy work and family relationships—because they are often wrong. True, people can be unkind, inconsiderate, oblivious, or downright mean, but it's rarely intentional. Most folks are too focused on themselves to intentionally try to provoke you. But because of the filter your brain has created from its previous history, it can be easy to believe they're doing it on purpose. Instead, try defaulting to the opposite assumption. Many people I've given this phrase to have turned all kinds of relationship challenges around simply by presuming goodwill on the other person's part. Even if someone does indeed have a nasty intention, which in my experience is relatively rare, the more we presume goodwill, the better the encounter goes.

Argue for their side

Do you find yourself in conflicts with others a lot? In situations where you are absolutely sure you are right and the other person is wrong—and you have no trouble saying so? Whenever I work with people like this, I notice that they end up in ping-pong arguments, tossing the ball of "I'm right"/"No, I'm right" back and forth, getting absolutely nowhere. It creates a stalemate unless one person has more power and pulls rank—"I'm the boss so we'll do it my way"—which may end the tug-of-war but doesn't help create buy-in or goodwill. I always suggest in these situations that my clients learn how to argue for the other person's side. Recently I came across the method social psychologist Anatol Rapoport suggested for creating a successful critical commentary. It's a great recipe for dealing with conflict. Rapoport believed that first you should reexpress the other person's position so well that they feel truly understood. Then you should list any points on which you agree and anything you have learned from what they said. Only then do you offer your perspective. Folks who use this habit changer to remind them to follow Rapoport's process are amazed to find that it moves them past conflict gridlock to much more collaborative possibilities.

Defenselessness
is your best
defense

A client of mine used to say he would only apologize if he ever did anything worthy of apology. The problem was he rarely believed that his actions were in fact apology-worthy. When I interviewed his coworkers, I was not surprised to learn about situations where others were offended not only by his words but more so by the fact that he could never admit he was wrong. In reality, all he had to do was apologize for causing hurt or frustration. Just like that, they would feel better *and* he would get credit for the apology. But he was extremely resistant, and so bad will increased between them. It took quite a while but eventually I helped him see that his greatest defense actually lay in being undefensive. If someone says you hurt or wronged them, I said, apologize without defensiveness: "I'm sorry I offended you." Because if someone feels offended, that's his or her reality, and it makes no sense to argue against another person's reality. Because the more you defend, the greater the offense becomes in the other person's mind. When you don't defend yourself, on the other hand, you don't get locked in to the "You did this"/"No I didn't" dynamic. My client agreed to try, using this phrase as a reminder. He found, to his surprise, that the result was much less conflict with those he worked with and therefore a greater willingness to collaborate with him. Try it if you need to be less defensive.

Remember
your
highest
intention

I was working with two friends who owned a business together. After years of harmonious partnership, they were having a lot of disagreements and requested that I mediate a conversation. To begin, I asked them what their highest intention was for the meeting. Both said some version of "To do what's best for our business and to preserve our friendship." I wrote it down on a flip chart so that they could see it, and we began to work. When the conversation would get heated or one person would get offended by what the other said, I would point to the paper to remind them of their intention. It helped them remember they both wanted the same thing for the business; they just disagreed about how to go about it. After that day, I worked on and off with them for about a year, and they used this habit changer throughout the process to recall in difficult moments what truly mattered to them both. Ultimately they decided to end their partnership, with one person buying out the other. But because they remembered their highest intention, they did it in such a respectful way that they remained friends.

In any challenging situation, when you get clear on your highest intention, it will help you call upon your best self to enact that intention. Maybe not always, maybe not perfectly, but more times than not!

Intention
and impact
are not one

This is one I give all the time to clients who speak without thinking about the effect what they are saying will have on their listeners. Folks like this tend to consider themselves "straight shooters" and "honest," which is undoubtedly true. The problem is that not thinking about the effect of words can also cause a lot of unnecessary conflict. This habit changer helps them remember that while their intention in what they are saying may be positive, the way it's landing on the other person might not have the effect they're looking for. It helps them to think about the *impact* as well as the *intention* of what they say. My clients also find it useful when communication with someone has broken down and an apology is necessary—because an apology is most effective when you express regret for the impact you caused *and* explain what your intention was. What's great about this slogan is that it also works in the reverse situation—when you're at the receiving end of a message that might sting. Separating the impact on you from the speaker's intention can help you go beyond your reaction to uncover the purpose he or she was aiming for. When you find the positive intention—*He was just trying to improve our process, even though it came across as devaluing what I've been doing for the past month*—it can help keep you open to working together in as positive a way as possible.

Decision
Making

D

Trust your inner GPS

client of mine was debriefing a situation at work. He had just realized that he'd made a bad hire and was now going to have to go through the painful and expensive process of terminating the person. "She looked great on paper," he said, "and the rest of the team really liked her during the interviews. I had a niggling feeling that something was not right, but I couldn't put it into words, so I let it go." This was not the first time I'd heard him talk about ignoring his gut. It seemed like he had good intuition but didn't trust it. I told him about a study I'd once read about people who had had brain surgery that left them with access only to logical, linear, left-brain thinking. Researchers thought it would be easier for them to make decisions than it is for the rest of us—they would just add up the pros and cons and decide logically, mathematically. But as experiments soon revealed, in reality the opposite was true—they couldn't make up their minds at all! Without access to gut feelings, they got lost in pros and cons. Our intuition often speaks in feelings, not words, but that doesn't mean it's not useful.

"Don't try to make decisions based only on facts—trust your intuition. You trust the GPS in your phone, don't you?" I asked that client. "Well, intuition is your inner GPS system." He began to use this habit changer to stop overriding his gut and, as a result, got comfortable not just trusting his intuition but acting on it—and immediately saw more effective results.

Think
beyond
either/or

I've either got to suck it up and stay here or quit my job and move out of the state," said Louise with a very unhappy look on her face. She was clearly not pleased with either choice. She was stuck on the horns of a dilemma. This is what happens when our brains bifurcate, meaning they perceive only two choices and waver between the two because neither is a great option. Bifurcation is such a common mental habit that we can get caught in! Louise was a master at it. Whenever someone is stuck there, I teach them a technique I learned from Native American author Paula Underwood. She said the Native Americans believe that if you haven't considered seven options, your thinking is incomplete. So I challenged Louise to come up with five other possibilities to deal with her problem. "They don't have to all be reasonable," I explained. "It's to break the deadlock in your mind and think beyond either/or." It was really hard for her, but she did it. And one turned out to be a solution that she liked much better than the two she'd been bouncing between. She was so happy that she adopted "Think beyond either/or" as her mantra every time she found herself bifurcating. This is a habit changer I've given out hundreds of times. In every decision there are always more than two choices. This will help you find them.

Delegation

D

Do what
only you
can do

Do you have trouble delegating? Believe in the old (misguided) maxim that if you want something done right, you'd better do it yourself? Or simply think it's faster to do it yourself than explain it to someone else? This habit changer is especially important for all you overdoers. To start, you need to remember that your talents, time, and attention are limited resources. This habit changer will help you distinguish what you should be doing given your job description, expertise, and abilities from what others can or should be doing. Do you need to be booking your own flights, or could your EA do it? Do you have to be on that marketing call, or would that be a great learning opportunity for one of your direct reports? You should be doing only what truly only you can do and letting others do what they are capable of! One of the high-performing executives I gave this habit changer to a while ago recently wrote to me. "My life is completely changed," she gushed. "I delegate a lot more now—to my assistant, to my employees—and I say no without guilt. I'm now spending less time on things that don't matter and more on what does. I thought the world would fall apart if I didn't do everything, but it's actually running more smoothly."

Ask yourself, what is it that only you can do in your role? Make sure you're doing only those things and not the things others can or should handle.

If they could, they would

Do you feel like a broken record when talking to folks who work for you—saying the same things over and over without seeing any real improvement? This is one of the most common issues I come across in supporting people who lead teams. It sounds like this: "I keep telling him to come to me if there is an issue, but he never does" or "I keep asking her to take more initiative, but . . ." If phrases like these sound familiar, this habit changer is for you. But to make this habit changer work, you have to realize that if you keep telling people something over and over and they aren't changing their behavior, you're just wasting your breath—if they *could* do what you're asking, they *would*. I first learned this the hard way when I ran my own company and had an employee who was a great worker but a terrible communicator. At every performance review there I was, telling him he had to let me know when he got overloaded, and he never did. Finally I realized that, rather than saying it again, I had to either help him learn how to know when he was overloaded and communicate that information or be more proactive myself in understanding his workload.

If you've made a suggestion or demand twice and a person's behavior hasn't changed at all, it's time to remember to stop telling and go into brainstorming mode with the individual in question: "Obviously this isn't working. What else can we try?" "How can I help you learn this?" etc. This will help you stop beating your head against the wall and get better results.

Fear

Handshake
your fear

Whether you're generally anxious or find yourself afraid in particular circumstances—like public speaking or when expressing opinions to important stakeholders at work—fear can be debilitating. Not only can it keep you from realizing your goals, but it can also prevent you from simply enjoying your day-to-day life. I know because I was ruled by fear for decades—and I'm not alone. This is an issue many people talk to me about. Part of the problem is that in Western culture fear is something we're generally taught to ignore or suppress; when we can't, we get even more overwhelmed. The Buddhists have a different approach. They suggest you befriend your fear, turn toward it as you would toward someone you loved who was feeling afraid: "Oh, you poor thing, I see you are afraid. You're not alone. I'm right here with you." In saying this you give your fear attention, neither ignoring it nor making more out of it than there is. It sounds backward, but oftentimes, paying attention to a feeling can make it lessen or even disappear. These words can also help you to see that you're more than your fear. Yes, there is the scared person inside you. But there is also the bold, wise part of you. Getting in touch with that wiser, braver self helps you act from confidence rather than fear—act not out of fear but *in spite of it*.

Go down
to the base
of the tree

When you're facing a scary situation— for instance, a divorce, a difficult medical diagnosis, the prospect of having to change careers—it's easy to feel swamped by your fear and let it rule your mind to the exclusion of everything else. You're not imagining that focus on the negative—that's actually the brain narrowing its area of awareness to make sure you pay attention to the possible danger rather than ignoring it. The downside is that this mechanism causes you to lose all perspective on the bigger picture. Going down to the base of the tree is a practice from Buddhist monk Thich Nhat Hanh designed to broaden our field of vision. In a windstorm the top of a tree may be blowing violently, but at the base it's unmoving. By looking at the "tree" in its entirety, we see its strength, solidity, and security. I recommend clients use this phrase to reconnect to the positives in their lives. For instance, a client of mine has a diagnosis of a serious health condition that threatens her ability to work full time. Using this mantra helps her remember that she has a family who loves her, money in the bank, a roof over her head. She repeats this mantra as many times a day as she needs to stay out of panic. It helps instill a sense of rootedness and relief that gives her comfort in the midst of fear. May it do the same for you if you need it.

Happiness

Reach for the better thought

Are you by nature a negative Eeyore—and tired of being that way? All kinds of research by positive psychologists over the past fifteen years shows that if you think pessimistic, hopeless, resentful, angry thoughts, you'll feel unhappy. So if you want to be happier, think happy thoughts, right? It's not so easy. If you've habitually been pessimistic, the magic doesn't happen on its own. You have to work at it. That's why I coined this habit changer for my clients who want to be happier. You have to *reach* for the better thought. It's not just going to come on its own. If you've habituated your mind to notice the bad, you've got to work to find the good. Ask yourself: What can you appreciate right now? What could the upside be? How might this turn out well? How can you contribute to a positive outcome? Remembering to reach for thoughts like these takes a lot of effort at the beginning, but I can tell you from working with lots of folks, you *can* train your brain to be more positive. Don't just take it from me: Martin Seligman, the father of positive psychology, proved it in the research he described in *Learned Optimism.* The more you practice positivity, the easier it gets. But what I love most about this one is that when you challenge yourself to reach for the better thought, you're forced to figure out what that thought is. And then, voilà, you've done it!

Change it, leave it, or accept it

Do you find yourself constantly complaining about a particular situation or person? Are your colleagues and friends tired of hearing you whine about it? Are you? To be happy, you have only three options when you find yourself in a less-than-ideal situation—you can change it, you can leave it, or you can accept it. That's it. Which will it be for you? My clients who use this phrase have found it extremely clarifying, whether dealing with a family or a work issue. Some have used it to improve their lot at work, to find a role, for instance, that's a better use of their talents and skills. Others have used it to conclude it's time to go and have moved on to other companies. Still others have learned to accept what's happening, to make peace with the situation. Many have tried one and then the other till they found the strategy that worked—and became happier as a result. I have to say, given the examples of the people I've worked with, that true acceptance is typically the most challenging, at least for high performers who are used to getting what they want through exerting more effort. Acceptance is an act of surrender, the opposite of effort. Nondoing. Nonetheless, you really have only these three choices—if you truly want to be happy, that is.

Patience

I have all
the time
I need

Lose your cool when the Xerox machine jams? When sitting in traffic? What about when you are trying to get out the door in the morning and your little ones are dragging their feet? Impatience is the curse of our modern era—the by-product of an ever more fast-paced world. We scare ourselves with the thought that we don't have enough time—to deal with this traffic jam, to listen to our daughter tell a story, to wait in this line.... And when you think that thought, because you don't have enough time you trigger the fight-or-flight response; it becomes a self-fulfilling prophecy. You end up not having enough time because you're operating in panic mode and therefore not using the time you do have wisely.

A super busy CEO of a $4 million start-up who had to wear many hats, from head of HR to marketing guru and office manager, found this phrase extremely useful. She'd find herself panicking when something would threaten to blow a hole in her schedule. Using this phrase helped her stay calm when an employee unexpectedly came to her door with a crisis or when a customer called out of the blue with a problem. She soon found herself better able to give her full attention to each situation and therefore was able to maximize her effectiveness. The more you tell yourself you have all the time you need, the more likely it is that you'll have the time you need!

Don't react
to your
reaction

Patience is defined, I believe, as the ability to stay cool, calm, and collected when things don't go your way. It's a combination of acceptance (this is what's happening), equanimity (I can stay unruffled with what's happening), and persistence (I can work through what's happening to get to a positive outcome). Some of us are better at it by temperament. Others are more high-strung and hard-driving and must train themselves to be patient. So how do you go about doing that? By using this habit changer. To begin, you need to understand that your impatience is at first an instinctive reaction—a tightening in the body, perhaps, or a thought such as *You are driving me crazy!* The problem is, if we're not careful, we can fall into the bad habit of expressing that inner reaction outwardly, lashing out with a mean remark, stomping off. . . . You know what your impatient response is! But you don't have to react to your reaction. Rather than react immediately, what you want to be able to do is take the time to respond in as skillful a way as possible. For instance, pause, then say, "I'd love to hear your story but have to be in a meeting in one minute. When can we talk?" When you work with this habit changer, you create a "time-out" that helps you consciously create the best response and prevents you from acting out of impatience even when you're stirred up inside.

Perfectionism

P

Relax,
you've
already
failed
at being
perfect

I first heard this phrase at a daylong retreat with the Buddhist teacher Jack Kornfield. Over the years, I've noticed he spends a lot of time talking to Westerners about how we need to stop trying to be perfect and accept ourselves as we are, warts and all. He's now using the phrase "loving awareness" to describe how we should consider ourselves and our actions. That's because the harder we try to be perfect, the more we beat ourselves up when we inevitably fall short, which results in our getting caught in a vicious cycle: attempted perfection, failure, castigation, renewed attempt, failure. . . . You know the drill. When instead we accept ourselves just as we are and hold ourselves in loving awareness, we're more mindful of what we're doing moment to moment and so are able to create the possibility of a new, fresh response. I recently had a conversation with a client who is using this habit changer. "It's made me be kinder to myself," he explained, "which I always believed would result in slacking off. But it's also helping me be more aware of what I'm saying and thinking moment to moment. My goal now is conscious action—whatever I do, I want to choose it with awareness." Awareness, as this leader discovered, is the greatest resource we have for changing anything. So stop trying to be perfect and instead try to increase your loving awareness of yourself. Ironically, it will lead you closer to perfection than perfectionism ever did!

Feed
forward,
not back

I once worked with a senior executive who alienated his staff by consistently complaining about all the little things people did wrong. No matter how well they did, no matter how large their accomplishment, he would find something to criticize: "Yes, you did bring in a hundred-thousand-dollar deal, but there is a typo on page twenty-seven." It was extremely demotivating, and as a result, he had a lot of employee turnover. I understood that his intention was to create excellence—that's the impulse underlying perfectionism—but it was backfiring. So I suggested that he use the slogan "Feed forward, not back." This idea comes from a term coined by leadership coach Marshall Goldsmith. Goldsmith rightly realized that there is a fundamental problem with feedback—it focuses on the past, which can't be changed. With feed forward, on the other hand, you don't comment on the past but simply make suggestions for improving performance in the future, such as "Next time, how about if you have someone proofread your copy before sending it to me?" If you are great at seeing what people haven't done right, consider expressing it in ways that can help them improve their performance in the future, so they can get even better, rather than feel shamed by past errors that can't be corrected. Your quest for excellence will be enhanced by this course correction.

Prioritization

If everything is a priority, nothing is

I was recently having a very common discussion with one of my clients, who was bemoaning the challenge of having too much to do and not enough time to do it. Is there any one of us in the work world today who doesn't struggle with this one? When I reminded him that he had to make sure to do the important things and learn to be okay with dumping, delegating, or deferring others, he remarked that it reminded him of something a mentor of his once said: "If everything is a priority, nothing is." "He taught me that it was my job as a manager to figure out what was truly important and work on that," my client explained. "I know how to do that. I'd just forgotten!" I looked at him and said, "So that's what I want you to say to yourself at the start of every day." "I can do that," he replied. And so he did. It helped him to sort through all the demands, problems, and requests coming at him and focus on those things that would make the biggest difference. I suggest you give it a try. It will help you cut through the noise to understand what you truly should be prioritizing. Of course, prioritizing may mean negotiating with others to get on the same page, but not letting everything be a priority is the way to ensure that what's most important gets done.

Hard
thinking
first

Do your days get so full of meetings, e-mails, and texts that by the time you get to the more substantive stuff you can't think? This is one of the most frequent issues my clients encounter. For instance, Monique had to come up with a new solution to a big company problem. "But I can never get to it!" she complained. "I need quiet, uninterrupted time and I'm too tired at night." I explained to her that the best time for thinking was the morning because the prefrontal cortex, the "executive function" of the brain, is like a battery that gets drained over the course of the day and is recharged by sleep, among other things. That's why we should do hard thinking first, when our brain is at its best, instead of wasting that power on e-mails and conference calls. To do that, however, we have to reclaim those morning hours. My client soon realized that although there were days when she had early meetings that she had to attend, most weeks she could block off the first two hours of at least two days to think. It worked so well that "Hard thinking first" became the catchphrase she taught all her direct reports, and soon they began routinely holding afternoon meetings so that everyone would get morning thinking time. Whether or not you are the leader, you too can find ways to carve out early hours—on your commute, perhaps, or by closing your office door for a half hour.

Is the juice worth the squeeze?

Ted, the head of a $10 million company, brought me in to work with his leadership team. In interviewing his employees, I learned that everyone felt they had too many priorities to execute anything well. When I sat in on a meeting, I saw the problem clearly. The people on his team had a lot of great ideas and committed to virtually every project they came up with. But in saying yes to everything, Ted and his team were skipping a crucial step in thinking through an idea: analyzing the concept before racing to implementation. What would the idea cost in both people hours and dollars? How much profit could they realistically expect to make? How did it fit in with everything else they were doing? In other words, sure, they could do it, but was it worth doing? Because I knew Ted thought in metaphors, I said, "You've got to figure out whether the juice is worth the squeeze." I suggested he use this habit changer to help him pause and analyze when he came up with an idea. He loved the concept so much that he incorporated it into the agreed-upon behaviors for his whole team. Every time a person came in with a new idea, someone would yell out, "Is the juice worth the squeeze?" As a result, they got more focused and strategic, which not only helped his employees feel less frazzled and overwhelmed but also had a positive impact on the bottom line.

Problem
Solving

Hold on
tightly, let
go lightly

Whenever we try to solve a problem, we have to strike the right balance: committing to an approach and giving it enough time to work but not getting stuck in doing something ineffective over and over. It's easy to err in either direction, but neither is productive. One client of mine, Sally, had problems with commitment—she was a classic flitter. She would agree to try a technique for dealing with a problematic employee and then report two weeks later that it was useless because she had tried once and it didn't work. Bob, on the other hand, was an overcommitter. He had one way of dealing with folks—the hammer—and hammer is what he'd do, even in the face of much evidence that it wasn't very effective. I was struggling to find a way to help them both when I read a blog post from mediator and author Tammy Lenski that I turned into this habit changer: "When I'm teaching mediators," she wrote, "I like to tell them to choose an approach to a problem confronting them, then *hold on tightly and let go lightly*." Sally used this mantra to stick to her course of action longer; Bob, to let go sooner.

We need both commitment *and* flexibility in problem solving. While every situation is different, and it's impossible for me to tell you how long to try and when to give up, this habit changer will help you find the right balance between overcommitment and calling it quits too quickly.

Drop the story

One of the most useful things I ever learned about the brain is that it is structured to take in new information and make meaning from it—stories, conclusions, assumptions—based on filters from the past. It does this automatically, below our conscious awareness. Like everything else our brain does, this has an upside—we couldn't function well if everything coming in were new to us (in fact, there are theorists who believe autism is related to having a faulty filter). But there's also a downside: Our unconscious story can get in the way of our seeing the new information so that we can respond in a fresh way. That was what was happening to Franz. His small company's sales were tanking and he was convinced it was because he didn't have the right person at the helm. Why? Because years ago he'd swapped the role out and sales had gone up. He was churning through sales directors when I met him. "What would happen if you drop the story that your problem is caused by the sales leader?" I asked. "Hmm," he replied. "I'd have to look to other factors, like market forces." After some analysis he discovered the real issue—his products were not competitive anymore—and quickly made manufacturing adjustments to cut costs. Not wanting to make that mistake again, he started to use this habit changer to make sure he wasn't making unconscious assumptions that interfered with getting to the root causes of problems. Whatever problems you're faced with, this one can help you too.

Procrastination

All you
need is the
first action

I generally don't procrastinate, but I recall vividly when I first used this habit changer for myself. It was years ago and I needed a Web site. Each day I would write "create a Web site" on my to-do list and promptly ignore it. This went on for months. Then I read *Getting Things Done* by David Allen. In it, he says that when we're not doing something, it's often because we think we need to know all the steps, but actually all we need is the first one, because the first action will lead to the next and so on. That's why I was stuck, I realized. I had no idea what all the steps were in creating a Web site. So I asked myself, *What's the first action?* Instantly an answer came: *Call my friend Dave, who can tell me whom to hire to help me.* My inner stalemate was broken, and incredibly, my Web site was ready within a week. Since then I've taught this habit changer to dozens of people who are frozen because a task feels overwhelming. I suggest they stop thinking about the whole and just focus on the first action. This allows them to take that initial step, which alleviates their anxiety about the big picture. And this doesn't work only when getting started—once you get started, just modify this habit changer to focus on the action that's "next" rather than "first." No matter what the project is, you can do it, one action at a time!

Work is
the best
way to get
working

I've worked with a lot of writers in my career, both as an editor and as a coach. And I've written a lot of books myself. So I know that there is nothing worse than the blank page for triggering a severe case of procrastination. You don't have to be a writer to experience it—it typically arises anytime you have to start something from scratch. Suddenly your desk needs straightening, the office needs cleaning out, Facebook needs your attention.... The longer you put it off, the worse you feel and the more unable you are to start. That was what was happening to my client Max, a workshop leader and author. He kept avoiding writing his blog, which was one of the ways he attracted workshop attendees. It got to the point where his procrastination was limiting his income. I told him that it was my experience with procrastination that work is the best way to get working. So I suggested that he think about what small task he could do regarding the blog that would get the ball rolling. "Find a great quote on the subject," he said immediately. I too typically do that when writing, because it forces me to write something related to that thought, which gets me past the blank page. Max used this slogan not only to get going on his blog but also to eventually turn those blog entries into a successful book. Why not try it to get past any "blank page" you may be experiencing?

Relationships

Mind
the gap

Alex was a super smart client who hired me because he wanted to become a VP at his organization. When I interviewed his stakeholders, it became clear that he didn't have the support of senior leaders for his goal. Why? Because he was always on broadcast mode and not aware of the stultifying effect his speechifying was having on the people around him. "He needs to learn to read the room," as one person put it. Alex, like many of us, got so focused on what he wanted to say that he failed to pay attention to how it was landing. He was missing an aspect of emotional intelligence called social awareness, the ability to pick up the subtle nonverbal clues to what's going on inside other people. I was struggling with how to help Alex when I took a trip to London and spent many a moment in the Underground listening to the "Mind the gap" announcement meant to warn riders to avoid falling in the space between the train and the platform. That's exactly what was happening to Alex, I suddenly realized. He wasn't minding the gap between what he said and how it was received. He started to repeat this mantra before every meeting he attended to remind himself to pay attention to the effect he was having on his audience. As a result, he became much more socially aware and eventually did get the promotion he so desired.

Fluff
and tend
regularly

It was a voice I hadn't heard on my phone in a long time—a client I had worked with who'd gone on to a role as the CEO of a new company. "I need your help," he was saying. "I'm afraid I'm about to be fired by the board." As I asked questions, the problem began to emerge. He would show up for quarterly board meetings and report on results, which were minimal because he was in the building/investment phase of the organization, and the board would hammer him. I suggested that he needed to have premeetings with folks before the board meeting, especially with the chairman, to answer questions, ask advice, and create alignment. To find out their concerns, what they cared about. "Stakeholders need to be fluffed and tended regularly," I explained. "Think about fluffing a pillow." I have no idea where I came up with that phrase, but I'd been using it for years to describe the kind of relationship management that is crucial to business success, particularly the higher you go in an organization. "Fluff and tend?" he replied in a contemptuous voice. "Well, I guess I've got nothing to lose." And so he did it—with amazing results. Not only did the board turn around, but when his contract came up, they renewed it for an additional three years. Since then I've given this habit changer to many would-be executives to help them remember that regular maintenance of crucial relationships is a critical job requirement.

Bringing them along is part of my job

Over the years, I've worked with a slew of high-powered executives who get to a certain level in their careers and then struggle building a followership. They often receive feedback that people can't track their thinking, that they don't connect the dots for people, that they move too fast. What I've come to see is that this is partially because they are rapid processors. Their minds work really fast—got it, now move on—while other people need more time and information to digest an idea and understand its implications in order to get comfortable with it. In other words, these clients needed to slow down, understand other people's pace of processing, explain more fully, and ask questions to create alignment and followership. I would explain all this to my speedy folks, but it wasn't till the manager of my client Rachel said to me that Rachel needed to understand that bringing people along was part of her job that I found the habit changer that would help. Rachel used it to remember to increase her patience and decrease her speed. Within six months she was getting remarkably different feedback about her value to the organization. Use this if you're annoyed at people "not getting it."

Recognition
and Reward

What gets
rewarded
gets done

This is a habit changer I recommend all the time to leaders who are not good at praising their people. Because they have a tremendous drive to achieve that fuels their every waking moment, such folks often don't appreciate how much positive feedback can improve performance, even theirs. In fact, according to research by the Gallup Organization, weekly praise is one of the twelve key factors driving higher productivity and profitability in organizations. That's because, below conscious awareness, the brain works for the hit of the feel-good hormone dopamine that praise provides. That's how it knows it's on the right track. If it doesn't get that hit, it assumes what it's doing is not worth the effort and stops trying so hard. But in order to work, praise needs to be specific—"Good job, guys" doesn't cut it because the brain doesn't know what specifically it did and thus what to repeat. This habit changer worked wonders for a leader named Marco, who declared recognition a "waste of time" when we first met. He came from the "stick" end of the carrot-and-stick motivational style. Once he learned the science of praise, though, he used this habit changer to remember to specifically call out what folks had done well during his one-on-ones and leadership team meetings. Amazingly, he found that over time he saw people achieving results he'd been hounding them for previously, and soon had little need for the stick.

If you don't ask, you don't get

re you someone who puts your head down, works hard, and expects the results you produce to get you the recognition and rewards you deserve? If so, good luck with that. I can't tell you how many people like that I've met—people who wait patiently to get promotions and raises, only to see their colleagues who are good at self-promotion vault ahead of them. Especially in large organizations, to get ahead you've got to ask for what you want and enlist influential people around you to help. Cynthia was such a person who thought her work should speak for itself. As a result, she'd been stuck in the same position for years. She used this habit changer to push herself out of her comfort zone, go to her manager, Ramon, and declare that she wanted to become a director. What did she need to do to make that happen? she asked. Together she and Ramon plotted out a strategy that involved taking the lead on a cross-functional project that would give her a lot of exposure as a leader to key stakeholders, as well as reaching out to high-level employees to ask for mentorship and guidance toward her goal. Within a year, she had the promotion she'd coveted.

The point is, you'll rarely get what you want if you don't ask for it.

Regret

R

Spilled
water is
hard to
gather

This one is a Chinese proverb I read in the novel *The Last Chinese Chef* by Nicole Mones. It's similar to the American expression "No use crying over spilt milk." But I like it better because it stresses the wasted effort that regret creates. Once you've learned what you can from whatever happened that you feel regretful about, continuing to focus on "if onlys" is truly torturous and useless mental effort. That was what one client of mine, Rita, was doing. She'd dropped out of the corporate rat race to raise her kids and was now finding it difficult to get back in the game. When I met her, she was so stuck regretting the decision she'd made ten years ago that she could see no way forward. She needed to put her energy toward creating a future she could enjoy, rather than beat herself up for her past choices. We worked on what kind of job she wanted given her talents, passions, and experience, and she created a game plan to achieve it. It was a departure from the career she'd had in the past, but it was something she believed would be fulfilling. Then she used this habit changer to stop herself every time she caught herself in regret and instead put her mind on going toward what she wanted. It took time and effort, but eventually she found a satisfying position.

Learn,
not churn;
then
change the
channel

Are you a ruminator? Do you go round and round about what you should have or could have done and have trouble letting go of self-recrimination? Do you constantly sabotage your happiness by "putting yourself in the blender and hitting 'high' and 'chop,'" as my friend fitness guru Dr. Pamela Peeke puts it? If so, this phrase can truly be a life saver to stop the mental churning. Here's how to use it: First take your questions seriously—your mind is trying to learn for the future. Whenever I hear a client asking, "Why didn't I?" or "Why did I?" I always stop and ask them to answer that question in a kind and curious—rather than self-deprecating—way: Why *did* you or *didn't* you do this thing? Next ask yourself what you'd like to do differently when faced with a similar situation in the future. Once you learn from your mistake by asking yourself these two questions, change the channel on your inner broadcast station and give yourself something else to think about or do. Then, every time you find yourself beating yourself up over this issue, think, *Change the channel,* and distract yourself. Give yourself something fun or really interesting to think about. One client of mine used this habit changer to stop obsessing over something she'd done ten years earlier. Imagine how freeing it is to know that you *can* take charge of your thoughts!

Resilience

R

Look how far I've come

This is a strategy long-distance runners use to resist the temptation to give up when they're tired or in pain. Scientists call it the horizon effect. Rather than focusing on how far they still have to go, they encourage themselves to keep at it based on the progress they've already made. When I have clients with a tendency to focus on their mistakes when they're learning a new behavior, I give them this habit changer to help them cultivate the resilience to keep at it. Because of the brain's tendency to be Velcro for the negative and Teflon for the positive, as neuropsychologist Rick Hanson describes our inborn negativity bias, when people encounter a minor setback, they often lose sight of the progress they've made. I'll never forget the client who called me to say she was a "total failure" at managing her anger because she'd stomped down the hall after a meeting. She was ready to give up on her anger-management efforts altogether. I reminded her that it was the first time she'd lost her temper in three months, whereas before it had been a weekly occurrence. Once she adopted this habit changer, it helped her stick to the techniques she'd found useful. Plus it helped her get back on the horse when she messed up, because she was able to see it as just an occasional slipup rather than a fundamental failure. Use this mantra when you need help sticking to whatever it is you're working on.

This is the end
of something
and the
beginning of
something else

When facing a profound loss—of an identity, a job, a business, a relationship—it can be hard to believe there will be a tomorrow worth living. The grief and sense of hopelessness can feel endless. Whenever I have clients in this painful place, I suggest this habit changer, which comes from my friend author Dawna Markova, PhD. It reminds us that whenever we experience an ending, we are also standing on the cusp of something new, which helps tremendously to create perspective and hope. I like it better than "When one door closes, another door opens," because it implies that it is from the death of what you have lost that the seed of the new will be born. It reminds us that nothing we have ever done is wasted—it's all compost for whatever is growing beneath the surface. Recently a client of mine used this mantra to help him make the hard choice to pull the plug on the start-up he'd invested his heart and soul in for two years. Within a week, he'd come up with a variation on the original idea, one that all his advisers agreed seemed to have more potential to be profitable. This kind of "rebirth" doesn't always happen so quickly or easily, but as this man discovered, the new has a way of emerging from the ashes of the old, even if we can't see how or when. Repeating this phrase to yourself in times of loss or transition will help you get from here to there.

It's not just
me this is
happening
to

Whenever we go through something difficult, it's easy to feel alone, like we're the only ones who have suffered this way. It's a natural tendency of our minds, as far as I can tell, and causes an anguishing sense of isolation and shame. What have we done that's so bad to deserve this unique form of punishment? This habit changer, which I actually picked up from a client in a powerful moment while he was going through a distressing layoff, is a great antidote to this tendency to take things personally. "It's not just me this is happening to," he said. "Many people are dealing with the same thing." That recognition made him feel less alone, and he used "It's not just me this is happening to" throughout the negotiation of the terms of his leaving, as well as throughout the process of finding another position. I noticed that the more he used it to get through his own challenge, the kinder he was not only to himself but also to others. Self-compassion researcher Kristin Neff calls what he was doing "recognizing our common humanity." Other phrases Neff suggests using when we're going through a painful situation: "Suffering is a part of life," "I'm not alone," "We all struggle in our lives." It's a wonderful way to increase both your self-compassion and compassion for others when dealing with something challenging.

I am like
the willow;
I will not
break

You *can* survive the challenges of your life even if it sometimes feels impossible. You can be strong, like a willow that bends but doesn't break. I've used this habit changer since I was a very young child dealing with a raging alcoholic mother and an absent father. I grew up in a house in the woods, and whenever I'd find myself in pain or fear, I'd lie in my bed and look at the willows outside my window. I realized that though they blew wildly in rain, wind, and snowstorms, their pliancy meant their branches never snapped off the way those of the surrounding pines and oaks did. I vowed to do the same and have used that phrase to get through not only my childhood difficulties but also many later challenges such as chronic pain, financial losses, and divorce. It's helped me not merely to be resilient but to actually experience the strength of my resiliency. Recently a client who's an entrepreneur going through the loss of funding for her business used it not only to get through the emotional challenge of that disappointment but also to bounce back quickly with a new idea. Another client drew a picture of a willow that she put up in her office to remind her to use the phrase whenever she got upset about problems with her teenage daughter. The willow tree is one of the most powerful symbols of strength and resilience I know. May it comfort and support you when you need it.

Nothing is
permanent

I use this saying all the time, whether I am happy or sad," said a young client of mine when I asked her for her favorite habit changer. "It helps me remember when things are good to appreciate the moment, because it won't last forever so I better enjoy it while it's here. And when things are hard, it helps me keep in mind that I won't always feel as badly as I do right now." What a wise twenty-two-year-old, I thought. It wasn't until I was forty that I even began to understand this truth. I would get stuck in my negative feelings, convinced I was going to feel bad forever, which of course increased both the length and duration of my downward spiral. And without even being aware of it, I would dismiss opportunities for treasuring the good feelings when they appeared. You have to notice good feelings to appreciate them! Recognizing the truth of impermanence—that everything does and will change—is one of the keys to resilience because it keeps us from concretizing the difficult times and becoming immobilized. And practicing gratitude, which this habit changer encourages by helping us appreciate what's good, also fosters resilience because it gives us a wider view of our world. Yes, the challenge you're facing is happening, but there are also good things to notice, and in noticing them you feel a bit lighter, a bit stronger, a bit more confident in your ability to weather the storm.

Risk Taking

R

If you do something, something will happen; if you do nothing, nothing will

Yvan came to work with me because he was at a crossroads. He had climbed the corporate ladder very fast and had what anyone looking from the outside would say was a great career. There was only one problem: He didn't like what he was doing. And he was lonely—he had sacrificed any hope of a personal life to focus on work and was now, at age forty, facing the fact that the life he had created had no meaning for him. At the same time he was afraid to risk letting go of the familiar to chance finding something—and someone—new. What if it didn't work out? What if he gave up his cushy job and never found love or meaningful work? Maybe it was better to play it safe. I found myself saying to him something I'd read in a novel: "If you do something, something will happen; if you do nothing, nothing will." That got to him. "What would you do if you were willing to do something?" I asked. "Take a year off and move to Thailand," he answered. "I've heard of a program where you can volunteer in a rural school. That's always been of interest to me." So he used this habit changer to help him take that risk. And yes, he met a fellow American while there and is now happily married.

Stand where you'd rather not

I want to shake things up in my life," said Julie, a middle-aged client with a newly empty nest. "I feel like I'm in a rut, only doing things that I've already done. But I'm not sure how to take a risk. My default is to say no and not even think about possibilities." I understood what she was going through. It's so easy to fall into routines in our lives, doing the same thing day after day, with fixed ideas of who we are and what we like and don't like: "I don't like parties." "I hate brussels sprouts." "I could never ski." Pretty soon we're living in a tiny space of our own making. It may be comfortable, but on the flip side, it can get pretty boring. Julie wanted to challenge herself to stretch and grow, but with a default of "no," how was she going to learn to risk moving beyond her comfort zone? Then I remembered a sentence that I'd read in *The Rise* by Sarah Lewis. "How about if you practice standing where you'd rather not?" I asked. She loved the idea and used this habit changer to remind herself to take a risk when something came up that she would typically say no to. Since then she's assumed a new role at work, said yes to lunch with a guy she barely knew, and taken up salsa dancing, all things she would never have done before.

Reduce
the risk

This concept comes from Sallie Krawcheck, named by *Forbes* as one of the World's 100 Most Powerful Women and widely known as one of the most powerful women on Wall Street. Writing on LinkedIn about how she was able to take the risks she has in her life, including accepting the daunting roles of CEO of the newly formed Smith Barney and later president of the Global Wealth & Investment Management division of Bank of America, she relates how at each possible turn in her career, she realized that she was risking "public humiliation" if she failed but stood the chance of gaining tremendous influence and impact if she succeeded. "Reduce the risk" was her strategy for taking on the challenges rather than running from them. For her, as she relates it, that meant putting a strong team in place with talents and experience that complemented rather than duplicated hers. Use this habit changer to go toward what you want when everything in you wants to run from it. Reducing the risk for you might be having a financial cushion to fall back on if things don't work out as a start-up CEO; or keeping ties to your old community as you move to a new, unfamiliar place; or even just trying out a new hobby before committing totally. Whatever it is, using this phrase will keep your fear at bay, which will ensure not just that you go for it but that you succeed!

Self-Care

Taking care of yourself is part of your job

I 've lost count of the number of high-achieving clients of mine who confess that self-care always ends up at the bottom of their to-do list. It happened again yesterday. "I've got my life really nailed," a female executive said. "The kids are great, my work is going well. The only thing is that I'm not taking very good care of myself. Exercise has gone out the window, I'm eating lots of junk, and my sleep isn't so great either." Whenever this topic comes up, here's what I say: "No one ever told you, but taking care of yourself is part of your job. It's not optional. Because to succeed at work, you need high ongoing mental, emotional, and physical energy to do your best. If you keep ignoring self-care, eventually you'll perform at a subpar level." Of course, we all know we're supposed to take good care of ourselves. But we're too busy working. That's why I invented this habit changer. It gives high-achieving folks like you permission to take the time to focus on themselves. Because when you understand that taking care of yourself is really part of your job, you see it as the business priority it is. So make a schedule of self-care and stick to it, like many people I've worked with, including one client in charge of a billion-dollar business unit who used this habit changer to start making appointments with himself at the gym—and has since gone on to become a triathlete.

Don't turn
goof-ups
into
give-ups

Let's say you're using the previous habit changer, going along just great and taking care of yourself—hitting the gym, eating well, getting the recommended seven hours or more of sleep—and then something happens: The holidays arrive and you binge on dessert, or your mother gets sick, which knocks out your exercise routine, or you're feeling low, so you comfort yourself with sugary or fatty snacks—the list of things that get in the way and derail our best efforts is endless. It's times like this when this mantra comes in handy. Because no matter how much you try to take good care of yourself, you will mess up. What's the secret to *lasting* success? It's refusing to *give up*, despite how many times you *goof up*. That's what this habit changer will help you do. It will keep you from eating the whole box of cookies just because you ate one, motivate you to get back on the bike after you've skipped a week, etc. My client Lucy used to feel so bad about blowing her health routine that she wallowed in inertia and self-hatred for weeks. Now when she goes off the fitness wagon, she uses this phrase to remind herself that tomorrow is a new day. Self-care is a long game— what you do on any given day doesn't matter nearly as much as how you do over years and decades. Yes, you blew it yesterday. So what? Get back at it today.

Self-Confidence

S

Be a tiger,
not a kitten

I love this phrase—it comes from a reader of one of my books who e-mailed me for help. "I want to be a tiger, not a kitten," she wrote. This young woman felt like she was too much of a pushover—she wanted to become more self-confident. This is not an uncommon desire. Yet whenever I work with people to grow their confidence, I'm struck by the fact that they view it as some magical quality that descends out of the sky. They've often spent a lot of time doing affirmations like "I am confident and strong." In my experience, such generic phrases don't work because your brain doesn't believe them: *No, you're not*, replies the negative voice in your head. Instead you need to create self-confidence through action, which gives your brain concrete evidence to build on. This habit changer helps you do this through experiences where you act like a tiger *even if you don't feel like one*. Start with small, low-threat ones that will build your confidence to take bigger risks. Maybe you start by telling a friend you didn't like how she was talking to you, and nothing terrible happened, so now you feel confident enough to risk telling your boss you want a raise. This mantra can also help you figure out what actions to take in a challenging situation: *If I were being a tiger right now, what would I do?* When you continually challenge yourself to be a tiger, you will become one!

Undistort
the
distortion

This is an idea that Sheryl Sandberg wrote about in *Lean In*, and it's based on the fact that, according to many studies across a wide range of disciplines, women are plagued by much lower self-confidence than men. This unfortunate phenomenon shows up in various ways. For instance, women consistently judge their performance as worse than it actually is, while men judge their performance as better than it is. And when it comes time to apply for a job, women don't feel qualified enough to apply unless they match 100 percent of the criteria, while men throw their hats into the ring if there is a 50 percent match. Even when we understand this phenomenon is social, not personal, it can be very hard to change. In writing about it, Sandberg noted about herself, "I learned over time that while it was hard to shake feelings of self-doubt, I could understand that there was a distortion.... I learned to undistort the distortion." The words jumped off the page at me as fodder for a wonderful habit changer. Since then, women I've worked with have used it to recognize when they're doubting themselves and to act in spite of their self-doubt, knowing that if they waited until they felt self-confident, they would wait forever. As one woman who used it to start her own business put it, "It helps me remember my feeling of unworthiness is a lie so I don't have to listen to it as much."

I'm a
butterfly,
not a moth

Do you have a tendency to hide your light under a bushel? Are you afraid of standing out for fear of upsetting someone else? This is a common problem among women that keeps us smaller than we could be. Somewhere along the line you got the message that your doing well means another female—friend, mother, sister—will feel bad, or that drawing attention to yourself is dangerous in some undefined way. So you stay mothlike, hiding in the shadows in order to not threaten those around you—and they don't even thank you for it because they don't even know that's what you're doing! This is such a common issue that I once had a famous woman come up to me after a talk I gave because she wanted, as she said, "to shake the hand of a woman who can announce what she's good at to a roomful of people." To turn this tendency around, a client of mine came up with this habit changer for herself. She was tired of living as a moth and decided to risk showing her true colors. She used the habit changer to gather the courage to leave her safe corporate job and launch her own successful international consulting company, a process that required her to toot her own horn and advertise her talents. Since then, many of my other women clients have embraced it as their mantra to equally powerful effect. What will showing your specialness lead you to?

Be the boss

I've worked with several women entrepreneurs recently who struggled with being the boss. They took the big risk of starting their own companies but then found themselves second-guessing every move and seeking more and more help from advisers who inevitably contradicted one another, leaving them even more unsure of how to proceed. One woman, Anne, recently attended a start-up incubator where seventy-seven men, one after another, told her what she was doing wrong and what they thought she should do instead. But rather than help her, all it did was shake her self-confidence and increase her confusion. No matter what situation you find yourself in, it is tough to balance the instinct to get advice from others with following your own sense of what's right. Erring too much on either side is not good, and it is my observation that women tend to err on the side of giving too much weight to the advice of others. Repeating the mantra "Be the boss" can counteract that, just as it helped Anne remember that the company she founded was hers, and that she should give her inner wisdom as much credence as she was giving everyone else's. Not only did she use it to sort through the advice of the seventy-seven guys, but from then on she used it each time anyone told her what to do—which put her firmly in the driver's seat of her own success.

Stress

S

This is
only a
paper tiger

When you're stressed out about something, it can feel a bit like a ravenous tiger is about to devour you, right? The problem seems overwhelmingly daunting, and you don't see how you are possibly going to cope. But there *is* a way out—recognizing that what you are facing is only a paper tiger, not a real one. This doesn't mean that there isn't a problem, just that it's not one that threatens your life. Neuropsychologist Rick Hanson created this metaphor to illustrate the fact that the stress response was designed to save you from physical danger—like a tiger chasing you. But your amygdala, which is where the stress response originates, can't differentiate between a tiger and a traffic jam. So it responds as if a tiger were after you when you're only stuck in line, experiencing a flight delay, or anticipating an important presentation. Using this habit changer whenever you are stressed reminds your body/mind you're not in mortal danger so that you can calm down and figure out how to deal with that line, delay, or presentation. "This habit changer has been a life saver," one stressed-out client said to me recently. "It's made it possible for me to stop, figure out if there even is a problem, solve it when needed, and then proceed with my day more calmly."

Is this plane still flying?

World War II fighter pilots were trained to use this question to help them decide when to hit the eject button and bail out of the plane. The rule of thumb was this: If the plane wasn't flying, get out. If it was, stay and use your wits to keep going. I tell stressed-out clients to use this habit changer to help them tell the difference between a *true* emergency and one that they really don't have to stress over. Forcing yourself to check whether you are really in danger or not is truly the only way you can begin to calm down, because it forces you to prove to your amygdala that there is no immediate threat so that it will turn down the stress response. In one example a senior executive client of mine had a hair-trigger stress response to certain situations at work. The thought of a missed deadline, the possibility of not meeting the forecast for the quarter, even the very chance of something happening that he didn't want would send his stress response through the roof. As a result, his blood pressure was in the danger zone, threatening both his health and his performance at work. He used this habit changer to remind himself that the world wasn't ending just because a problem, or the potential for a problem, had arisen. At first he had to repeat it a lot every day, but he did learn to be calmer and his blood pressure responded accordingly.

Success

S

Since you will compare, compare well

I was talking to a twentysomething business owner who was complaining about not being "as far along" on the success path as her peers. This is a common feeling, right? We look around, rank ourselves on some invisible scale of achievement, and usually find ourselves wanting. There's always someone who's done more, made more money, gotten more glory, no matter our age and stage. Often happiness experts tell us that we shouldn't compare ourselves to others, but that's impossible—part of what our prefrontal cortex exists to do is take in information and compare that to conclusions and judgments it has previously made. What we *can* do about this tendency of our brain, however, as I explained to my young client, is to be sure to compare well. "What do you mean?" she asked. "Well," I said, "what does success look like to you?" She had her answer immediately: "Being my own boss, having the freedom to do things when and how I want." "So when you compare your situation to others given those criteria, what do you notice?" I replied. "I've already got what I want!" she exclaimed. "I've been so busy comparing myself against a yardstick I'm not even interested in that I didn't even notice the success I've created." Since then, she and other clients have used this habit changer to keep reminding themselves to orient toward the success they truly want. You can too! It will ensure you're comparing yourself by measurements you truly value.

To create success, focus on past success

I've worked with many successful people who had performance anxiety when it came to doing big presentations. In talking about it, they tended to focus on their fear of making a fool of themselves. I asked each of them one question: "Can you remember a time when you did a presentation that went really well?" Just as I suspected, each person could recall at least one time that, despite their anxiety, they did a good—or even great—job. Then I asked them to focus on that previous success: to see, feel, and hear themselves in that circumstance in as much detail as possible. What did they do to make it go well? How did it feel? Then I suggested that they use this habit changer to recall vividly their previous success each time they started to feel anxious, especially just before their next presentation. Each person said it helped a lot, but this slogan isn't just for presentations. It works for anything you want to do well. Focusing on previous success creates success because it helps us notice what we did right so we can repeat it: *Oh, yes, first I spoke to my peer to get her point of view, and then I was more prepared to talk to the larger group.* Conversely, focusing on failure tends to create more failure. Because of the brain's negativity bias, unless we remind ourselves with this phrase, we can easily get stuck on what we've done wrong, which disables our patterns of success.

Aspire without attachment

This is a habit changer that I often give to founders of start-ups who get so concerned about failing at their business that they make themselves and everyone around them suffer—and put their business at risk in the process. It's a concept that comes from neuropsychologist Rick Hanson, who differentiates between attachment, which is striving for your goals with stress and pressure not to fail, and aspiration, which is a going toward what you want with "outer effort and inner peacefulness, rewarded by the journey itself no matter the destination." I often suggest it to my most ambitious clients because I've observed that, as Hanson notes in his book *Just One Thing*, "paradoxically, holding your goals lightly increases the chance of attaining them, while being attached—and thus fearing failure—gets in the way of peak performance." This doesn't mean not being dedicated and disciplined about where you are trying to go, but rather not getting caught up to the point that you feel desperate about it. Hanson points out that there is a different brain system involved when we aspire, which is about *liking* (I prefer) and is normal, versus when we're attached, which is about *wanting* (I gotta have) and creates craving and unhappiness. Use this habit changer to help you work toward goals from a place of aspiration and, as Hanson says, "feel into the ways your life is and will be basically all right even if you don't attain a particular goal."

Work-Life
Balance

Don't worry, your to-do list is endless

This one's for you if you are someone who stresses about trying to get everything done and/or feels anxious that your to-do list is too long, your e-mail in-box too full. I promise you that *no one* gets to the end of the list or has an empty e-mail in-box—well, maybe for an hour or two, but it fills up again in a blink of an eye. We *all* have too much to do, and when you try to finish it all, you only put unnecessary pressure on yourself and cause yourself to work beyond the point of exhaustion. Doing the important work is hard enough—no need to add the extra pressure of presuming you should be superhuman. I've recommended this habit changer to dozens of people to help them stop beating themselves up over what is left undone. Recently a young father who saw his three-year-old only on weekends because he stayed late every night "to catch up" vowed to use this habit changer to leave work earlier twice a week to play with his son, which is restorative for him, as well as important for his child. He reported to me yesterday that he now has more stamina for work when he is in the office, and that his relationship with his son—and wife—is better than ever.

Busy is a
decision

This habit changer, an idea that comes from *Uncertainty* author Jonathan Fields, is one I give my high-powered clients who are pushing themselves past the point of strain. They "have to" go to India for two weeks for business, despite having been on the road for the past six weeks to the detriment of their health and marriage; they "have to" attend the off-site despite strict orders from the doctor to stay in bed for four weeks after surgery; they "have to" miss their daughter's dance recital for a late-night meeting (all true stories from my clients), and so on. Actually they're *choosing* to do these things. However, when you're in this state, it feels choiceless, doesn't it? Often it takes being stopped in your tracks to get the message. I learned this truth when I hurt my back in my early twenties and was totally bedridden for months. Somehow the world, and my life, went on even though I wasn't doing *anything* I absolutely "had" to do. Busy truly is a decision, and only when we understand that we are choosing it can we decide to choose otherwise. My India-trip client used this habit changer to postpone her trip for a month so that she could have time to recover and reconnect. The client with the dancing daughter found someone to listen in for him at the meeting. The postsurgery client sent his regrets. You *can* slow down, and your world will not come to an end.

Now turn
your bowl
over

Have trouble leaving work at work? Feel dissatisfied with your accomplishments no matter what you've done during the day? Many of my high-performing clients with fast, restless minds and a drive to achieve feel this way. That's when I suggest this habit changer. It comes from a story in *Kitchen Table Wisdom*. In that book Rachel Naomi Remen writes about a tradition of her Orthodox Jewish grandmother. In the morning she would fill a bowl with water and recite a blessing asking to live to her fullest that day. When the day was over, she would pour out the water and turn the bowl over, signifying that she'd done her best with the day she'd been given and now it was done. Those who use the mantra find it a useful way to separate work and rest time. Draw on it if you can't let go of the issues, problems, and challenges of your daily life and thus can get no satisfaction and little peace. Imagine you are holding a bowl filled with all that you have accomplished today—even if it isn't as much as you wished—then turn it upside down. You've done your best for today. You will take up the cares of the world again tomorrow. You'll do your best when tomorrow comes. Now it's time to turn your bowl over and rest.

Worry

Don't go in your mind where your body is not

Do you constantly worry about all the terrible things that *might* happen? Many of us torture ourselves with this brand of magical thinking: *If I worry now, it will help keep the bad thing away.* Actually all you do is make yourself miserable now as you focus on the prospect of misfortune and the unhappiness you will feel if it occurs, which it usually doesn't! If you're a chronic worrier, try this habit changer, which comes courtesy of an English-as-a-second-language client of mine. I was working with her to stop worrying about all the possible future catastrophes that could befall her and suggested that she say to herself, *I'll cross that bridge when I come to it.* Soon after that we came to the end of her coaching engagement and she moved on to an overseas work assignment. A couple of years later, she called me out of the blue to say how helpful it had been to learn to "not go in her mind where her body is not." It had completely eliminated her worrying. I was so delighted with her translation that now I give it to all my worriers. Use it to remind yourself that all worries are in the future and likely will not come to pass. You're not there yet—it's all happening in your mind. And if some terrible thing does indeed happen, you can deal with it when it arrives.

Outsource
your worry

A client of mine recently inspired this concept. She wasn't actually trying to get others to worry for her. What she was talking about was enlisting help, in this case from her assistant, to brainstorm ways to avoid issues that typically caused her worry: fear of being late and of not being prepared. But framing it as outsourcing her worry enabled her to get the assistance she needed. I loved this notion because each of us tends to worry in the places we need the most support. We are all strong at certain ways of thinking and not at others. We worry because we don't have easy answers in the types of thinking where we are not strong. For this client it was procedural thinking. For me it's thinking about the future. Because of our lack of ease in a particular area, it's easy to get stuck in the spin cycle of worry, not knowing what to do but somehow thinking we have to figure it out on our own. This habit changer is useful for reminding yourself when you're spinning to reach out to someone who's great at thinking in the way you need. For my client it was her assistant, who helped her create a schedule with set preparation time and enough space in it that she didn't have to fear being late. You don't have to figure it out on your own—outsource your worry!

ACKNOWLEDGMENTS

Every time I write a book, which leads me to reflect on what I do and how I do it, I am struck again by how much of my way of working comes from learning with and from my dear friend and mentor Dr. Dawna Markova, CEO emeritus of Professional Thinking Partners (PTP). Her groundbreaking work on how people think, learn, and communicate, as well as her asset-focused approach to human capacity, informs my thinking on a daily basis. My appreciation for her is boundless.

This book would not exist without the support of my brilliant agent Yfat Reiss Gendell and the rest of her stellar team at Foundry Media: Jessica Felleman, Kirsten Neuhaus, Jessica Regel, Sara DeNobrega, Heidi Gall, and Michelle Hammond. Yfat led me to the wonderful folks at Crown Business: the fabulous editor Talia Krohn; her assistant Dannalie Diaz; publisher Tina Constable; associate publisher Campbell Warton; assistant Jennifer Reyes; Megan Perritt and

Ayelet Gruenpecht, publicity and marketing goddesses; Megan and Ayelet's assistant Owen Haney; sales directors Christine Edwards and Candice Chaplin; special sales rep Daryl Mattson; cover designer Kalena Schoen; and copy editor Hilary Roberts. As a former publisher, I know what it takes to get a book out the door, and I wholeheartedly thank each one of them for doing their part to launch this book into the world.

A big thank-you also to Emily Miles Terry and Leslie Rossman of Open Book Publicity. They have been my publicists for longer than any of us would care to admit. I couldn't imagine doing a book without them.

I'd also like to offer a special thank-you to my friends and family who offered suggestions for habit changers and shared their stories: Ana Li McIlraith, Meagan, Laz, and Matthew Gonzalez, Stephanie Ryan, Beatrice Stonebanks, and Joey Magrino. I also want to acknowledge my clients, from whom I learn every single day. To protect confidentiality, they are not named in these pages. In fact, in providing examples, I've changed names and genders and altered circumstances. Even the quotes you've read reflect the spirit, not the exact words, of the conversation.

Finally, I am not a Buddhist scholar or teacher, nor even a very good student, but you will probably have noticed a Buddhist flavor running through this book. I give thanks to the teachings and to teachers

I have learned from, including Jack Kornfield, Pema Chodron, Thich Nhat Hanh, Sylvia Boorstein, and Rick Hanson. If you'd like to learn more about formal Buddhist slogan practice, two good resources are *Training in Compassion: Zen Teachings on the Practice of Lojong* by Norman Fischer and *Always Maintain a Joyful Mind: And Other Lojong Teachings on Awakening Compassion and Fearlessness* by Pema Chodron.

Want More Support in Creating Lasting Change?

For lots more tips, tools, and techniques, as well as the latest brain science on change, go to Habit-Changers.com.
You can also connect with M. J. on:

TWITTER: @MJRyan8

INSTAGRAM: mjryan4178

FACEBOOK: maryjane.ryan.71 or join her Facebook group on change, Change Expert: MJ Ryan.

If you're interested in individual coaching, you can e-mail M. J. at mjryan@mj-ryan.com.

Are you really ready to change?

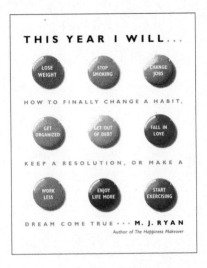

For anyone who has broken a New Year's resolution, fallen off a diet, or given up on fulfilling a dream, the ingenious strategies, inspiring stories, and sheer motivational energy of *This Year I Will* ... help you make a promise to yourself that you can actually keep.

Find your unique formula for planning, implementing, and succeeding from the leading expert on change and human fulfillment and bestselling author M. J. Ryan.